I got a new cell phone, but the first name in my address book is still Asada.
Argh.

-Tite Kubo

Bleach is author Tite Kubo's second title. Kubo made his debut with *ZOMBIEPOWDER.*, a four-volume series for *Weekly Shonen Jump*. To date, *Bleach* has been translated into numerous languages and has also inspired an animated TV series that began airing in the U.S. in 2006. Beginning its serialization in 2001, *Bleach* is still a mainstay in the pages of *Weekly Shonen Jump*. In 2005, *Bleach* was awarded the prestigious Shogakukan Manga Award in the *shonen* (boys) category.

BLEACH
Vol. 28: BARON'S LECTURE FULL-COURSE
SHONEN JUMP Manga Edition
This volume contains material that was originally published in English in SHONEN JUMP #78-80. Artwork in the magazine may have been altered slightly from what is presented in this volume.

STORY AND ART BY
TITE KUBO

English Adaptation/Lance Caselman
Translation/Joe Yamazaki
Touch-Up Art & Lettering/Mark McMurray
Design/Sean Lee
Editor/Pancha Diaz

VP, Production/Alvin Lu
VP, Sales & Product Marketing/Gonzalo Ferreyra
VP, Creative/Linda Espinosa
Publisher/Hyoe Narita

Printed in the U.S.A.

Published by VIZ Media, LLC
P.O. Box 77010
San Francisco, CA 94107

10 9 8 7 6 5 4 3 2
First printing, September 2009
Second printing, October 2009

PARENTAL ADVISORY
BLEACH is rated T for Teen and is recommended for ages 13 and up. This volume contains fantasy violence.
ratings.viz.com

My lord, we look at you
as we might look at
a Peacock

You are framed by something sublime
similar to
hope, worship and fear

BLEACH 28

BARON'S LECTURE FULL-COURSE

Shonen Jump Manga

STARS AND

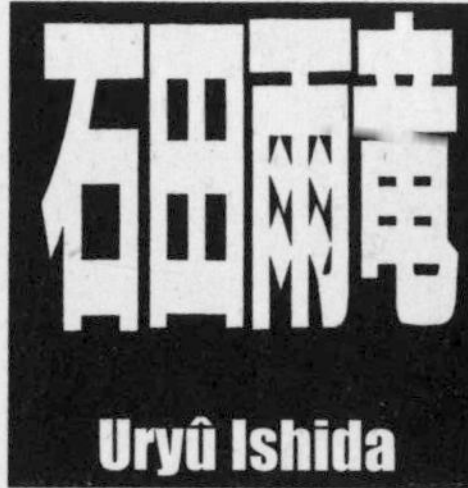

When high school student Ichigo Kurosaki meets Soul Reaper Rukia Kuchiki his life is changed forever. Soon Ichigo is a soul-cleansing Soul Reaper too, and he finds himself having adventures–and problems–he never could have imagined. Now Ichigo and his friends face their greatest challenge yet in the form of the renegade Soul Reaper Aizen and his army of Arrancars, who are bent on killing the king of the Soul Society and wiping out Karakura in the process.

As the Arrancar threat looms ever nearer, the Soul Reapers are recalled to the Soul Society and Ichigo is ordered to await further orders in Karakura. But with Orihime in enemy hands, Ichigo has other ideas.

BLEACH ALL

Orihime Inoue

井上織姫

STORIES

BLEACH 28

BARON'S LECTURE FULL-COURSE

Contents

243. The Knuckle & The Arrow

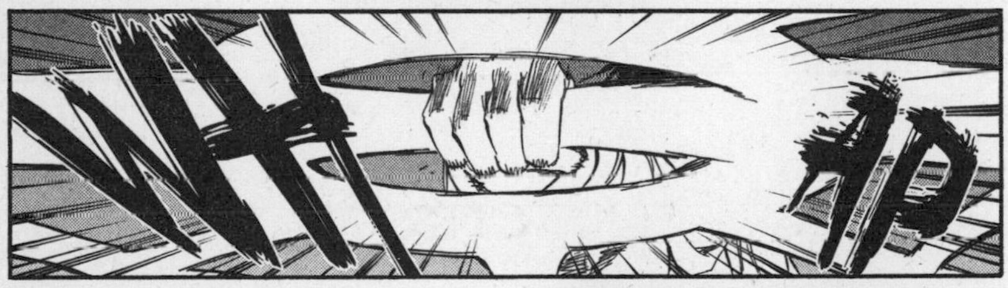

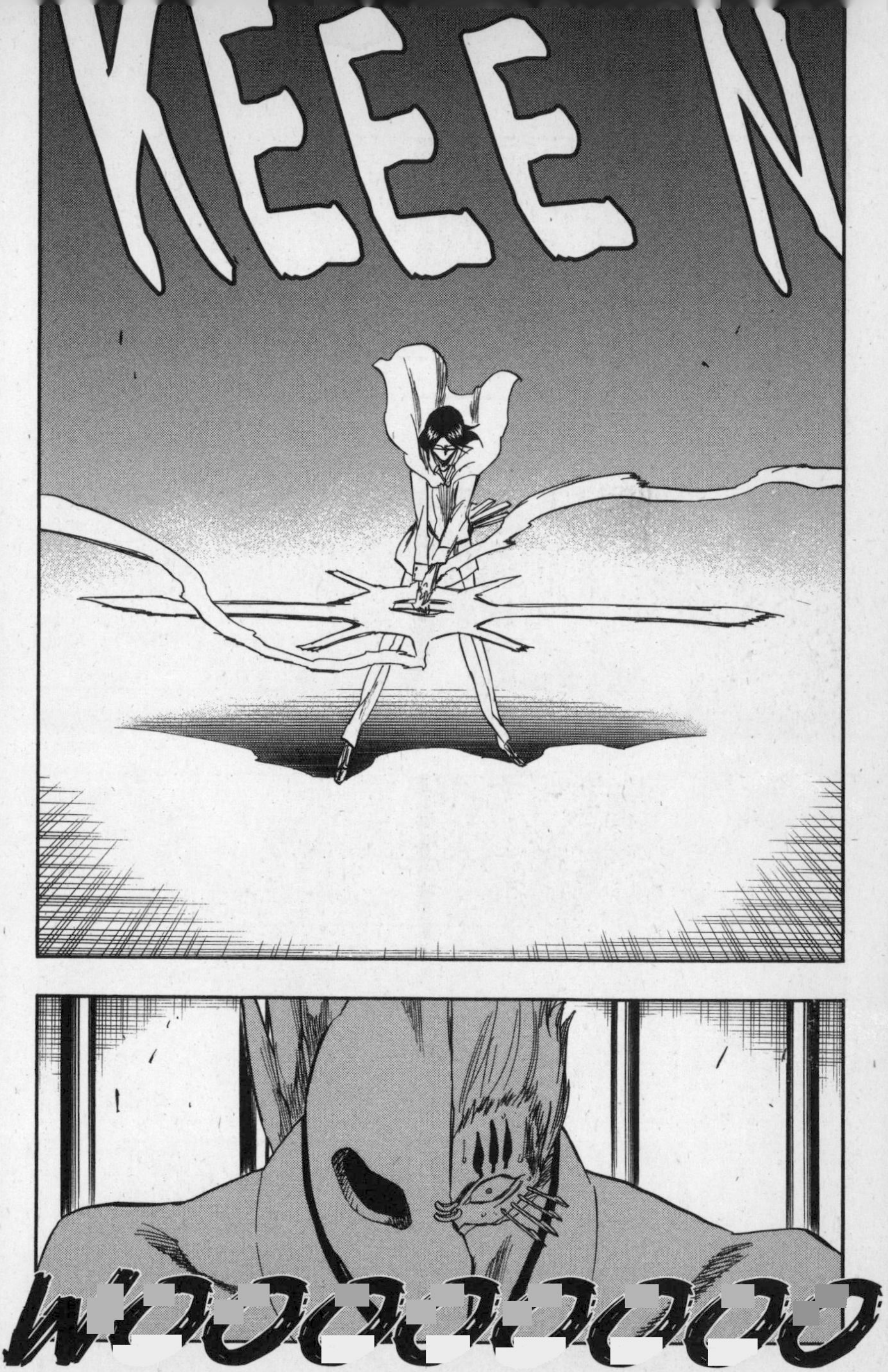

KEEE N

...GINREI KOJAKU.

(LONE SPARROW ON A SILVER CLIFF)

BLEACH 243. The Knuckle & The Arrow

KLAK KLAK KLAK
HUFF
KLAK
HUFF
KRUSH

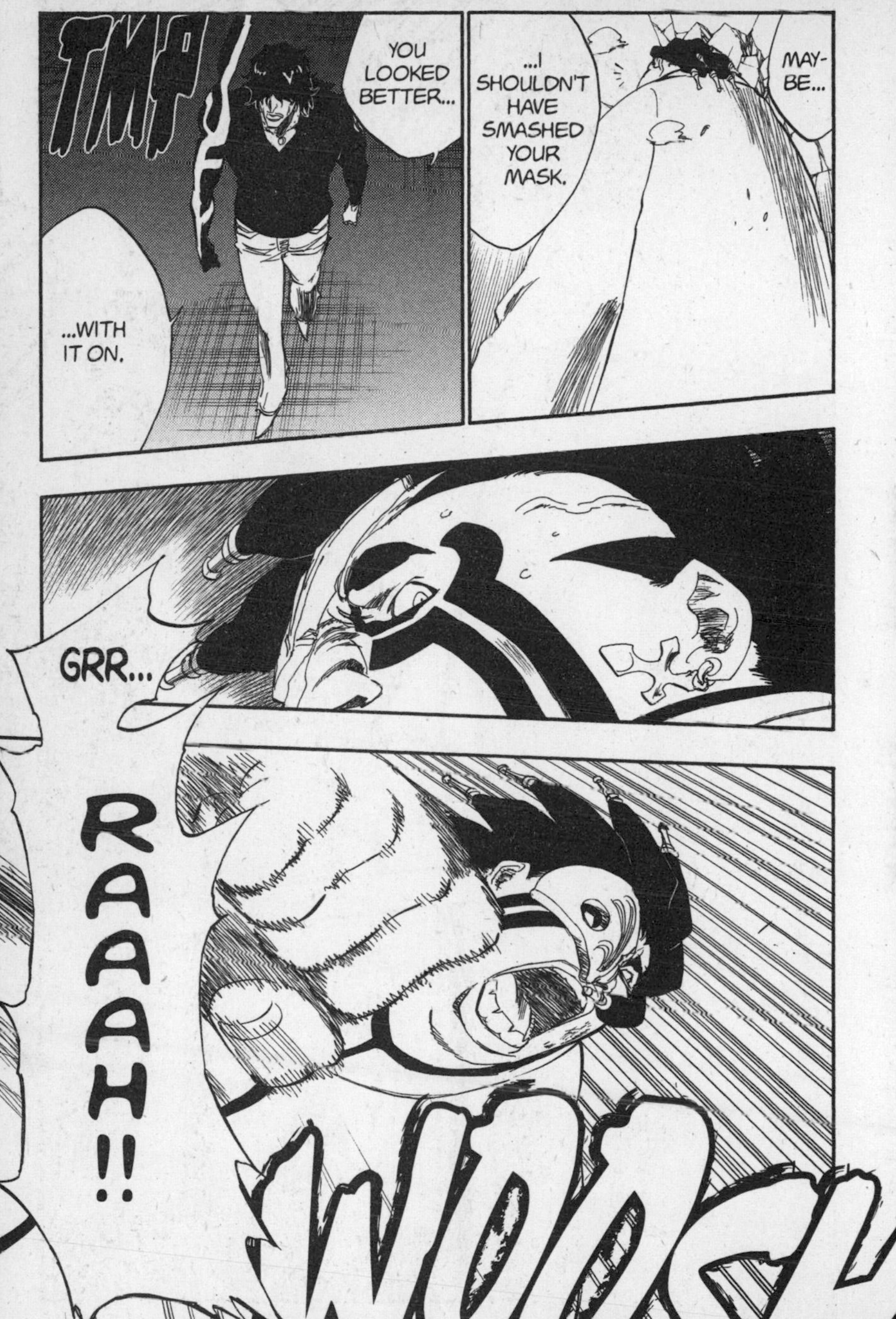
MAY-BE...
...I SHOULDN'T HAVE SMASHED YOUR MASK.
TMP
YOU LOOKED BETTER...
...WITH IT ON.
GRR...
RAAAAH!!
WOOSH

KREEK

KREEK

WHAT'S THE MATTER, TOUGH GUY?

THAT ALL YOU GOT?

KROOOM
SHOOM
HUFF
BLAST...
HUFF
STUPID HUMAN!
HUFF
IS THIS...
...WHAT YOU PEOPLE CALL A SONÍDO?
NOT BAD.
PRETTY FAST.
SHOOM
!
WHAT?!
A HUMAN KEEPING UP WITH A SONÍDO?!

THAT'S RIGHT.
BUT THEN, I'M NO ORDINARY HUMAN.
I'M A QUINCY.

THIS IS A QUINCY HIGH-SPEED TECHNIQUE. IT'S CALLED HIREN KYAKU.
WOOOOOOOOO
PERSON-ALLY...
I THINK IT'S FASTER THAN THE TECHNIQUE YOU AND THE SOUL REAPERS USE.

A QUINCY ?!
A SUPERIOR KIND OF HUMAN?!
NEVER HEARD OF THEM!

YOU HAVEN'T ?
HMM...
YOU SHOULD BE ASHAMED OF YOUR IGNORANCE.
WHUP
SHUT UP!!

SHWUP
THE FACT THAT YOU CAN KEEP UP WITH MY SONÍDO MEANS NOTHING!
UNLESS...
...YOU CAN STOP MY UÑA TIROTEA!! (CLAW WINGS)
FWOOM
ZHEEEN

FWO
OM

RRMMMMMMMMMM

HA!
SO YOU THINK YOU CAN SHOOT DOWN ALL MY TIROTEAS WITH ARROWS?
WHAT A SIMPLE-MINDED SOLUTION!
THAT'S SOMETHING A CHILD WOULD THINK OF, QUINCY!

GOOD LUCK!
BUT BE WARNED!
MY UÑA TIROTEA FIRES 108 MISSILES AT ONCE!
I'LL JUST SIT BACK AND WATCH YOU...
IS THAT RIGHT?
THEN LET ME WARN YOU...
MY GINREI KOJAKU FIRES...

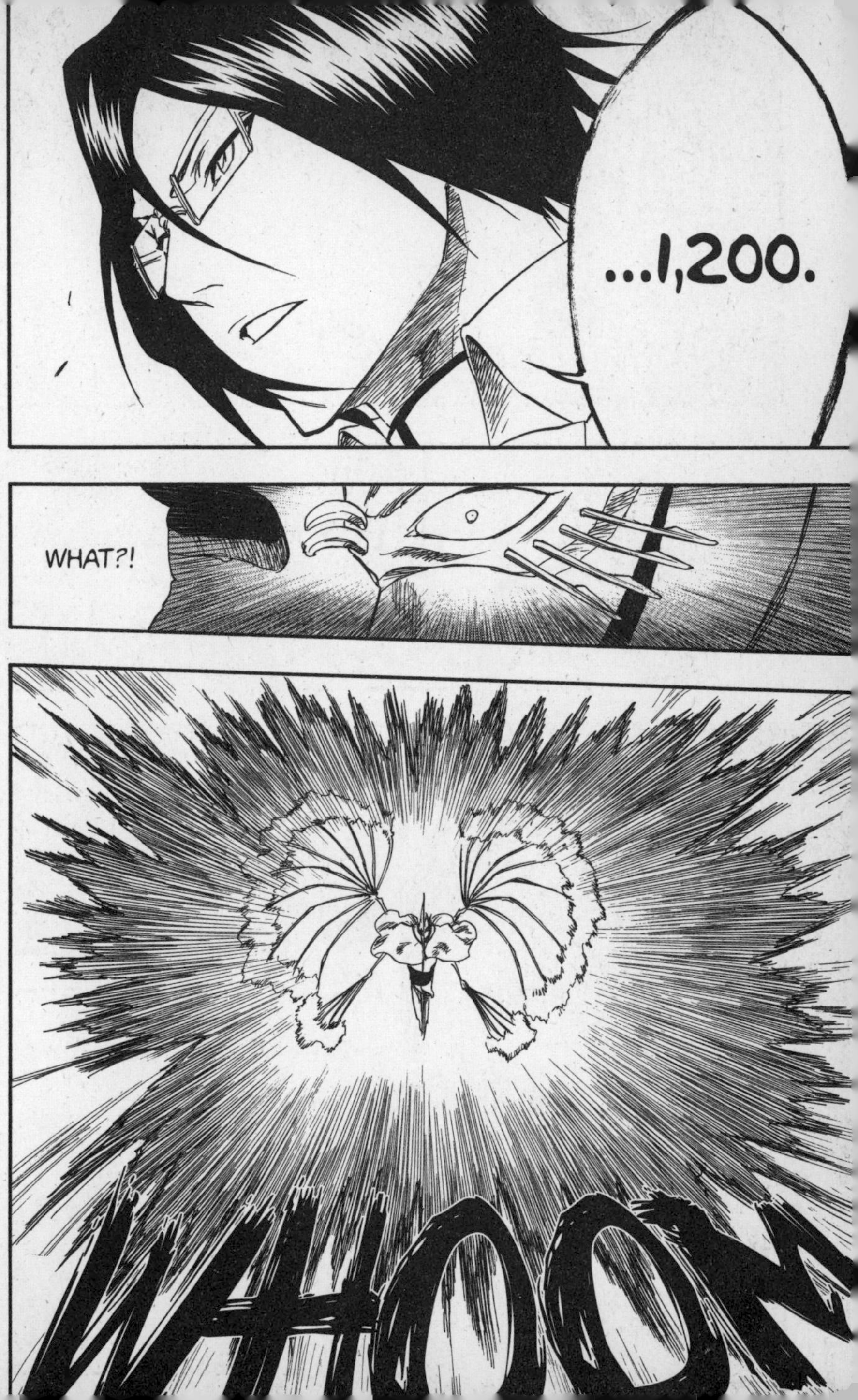

WHOOM

RRMMMMMMMM

THUD
HUFF
HUFF
HUFF

TMP

...DE-
FEAT
ME!!

RATS ...
YOU LOUSY ...
THERE'S NO WAY I CAN...
...LET A WIMP LIKE YOU...

SHOOO
THWAP

KRUMP KRUMP KRUMP
KRASH

THOO-M
NGH...
NO...
...WAY.
ARE YOU DONE?
THIS LOOKS TO ME...
KA-CHAK
...LIKE AN ATTACK OF LAST RESORT.

ALL RIGHT.
NOW IT'S MY TURN.
FWOOOO
SORRY.
NORMALLY...
TMP
...I DON'T ENJOY FINISHING OFF AN ENEMY WHO'S LOST HIS WILL TO FIGHT, BUT...
TMP
TMP
UNH... UGH...
I THINK THIS TIME...
...I CAN'T AFFORD TO BE NICE.
TMP

EL DIRECTO.
(GIANT'S STRIKE)

SO MR. KUROSAKI IS OFF TO HUECO MUNDO, BUT...

...THAT DOESN'T MEAN THERE WON'T BE ANY HOLLOWS SHOWING UP IN KARAKURA!

I HAVE TO DO SOMETHING ABOUT THEM, BUT I HAVE OTHER URGENT MATTERS TO ATTEND TO AS WELL.

BUT I HAVE A PLAN!

AGH

GACK

244. Born From The Fear

IT'S OVER.

KLAK

KROOSH

SHRUFF
UGH...

KREEK
BLAST THAT...
...STUPID ...HUMAN...
SHO OM

I TOLD YOU-- I'M A QUINCY.
NOW I WANT YOU...
...TO GIVE AIZEN...
...A MESSAGE FOR ME.

TELL HIM A QUINCY IS HERE.

TELL HIM IT'S NOT THE SOUL REAPERS HE SHOULD FEAR...

...BUT THE QUINCY!

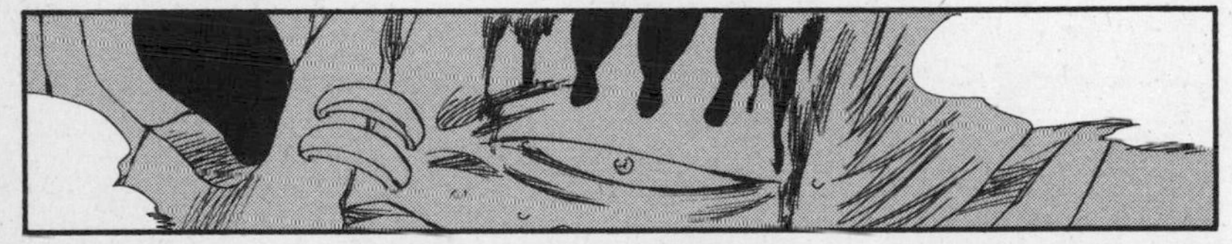

REMEMBER THIS, HUMANS!
THAT'S THE KIND OF ENEMY YOU'RE UP AGAINST!
THE BATTLE ONLY **BEGINS** HERE.
AND THERE IS NO VICTORY...
...WHERE YOU ARE GOING.

LET'S GO!
UP THE STAIRS!
RRMMMMMMM

HE SHOULD FEAR YOU...
...EH?
THAT'S A BOLD STATE-MENT, QUINCY.

BUT YOU DON'T UNDERSTAND.

LORD AIZEN...
...FEARS NO ONE.

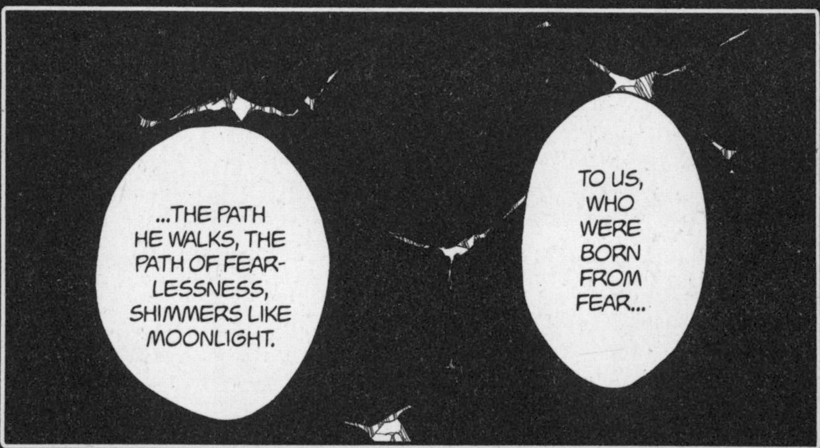

BLEACH 244. Born From The Fear

RRMMMMMMMM

KRO

HWAAH!!
FWOOM

HUFF
HUFF
WELL... WE MADE IT OUT SOME-HOW.
HUFF
HUFF
SO THIS... ...IS THEIR WORLD.
THERE HAS TO BE A WAY OUT.

THIS...

...IS HUECO MUNDO.

IS IT A PALACE ...
OR A FORT-RESS?
IS THIS LAS NOCHES, THE PLACE THAT GUY WAS TALKING ABOUT?
IT'S HUGE!

LOOK.
THE TREES LOOK LIKE STICKS NEXT TO IT.
IT MUST BE ENOR-MOUS.
IT'S MESSING UP MY SENSE OF SCALE.

GOOD THING WE GOT TO SEE IT FROM A DISTANCE SO THAT WE COULD GET A PICTURE OF THE WHOLE AREA.
WHAT GOOD DOES THAT DO US?
IT MIGHT BE USEFUL LATER.
IT'S BETTER THAN NOT SEEING IT, ANY-WAY.
WELL ...
I'M WILLING TO BET THAT ORIHIME'S IN THERE SOME-WHERE.

PROB-
ABLY
SO.
THERE
DOESN'T
APPEAR TO
BE
ANYWHERE
ELSE THEY
COULD BE
HIDING
HER.
YOU
GUYS
READY
TO
RUN
?
IF WE STAND
AROUND
HERE, WE'RE
JUST ASKING
TO BE
ATTACKED.
YEAH.

TMP

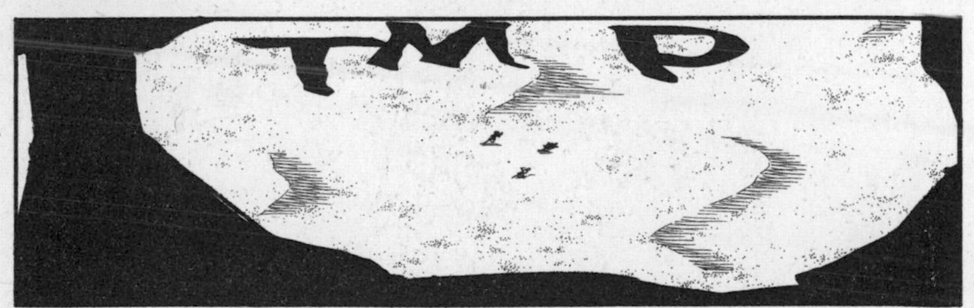
TMP

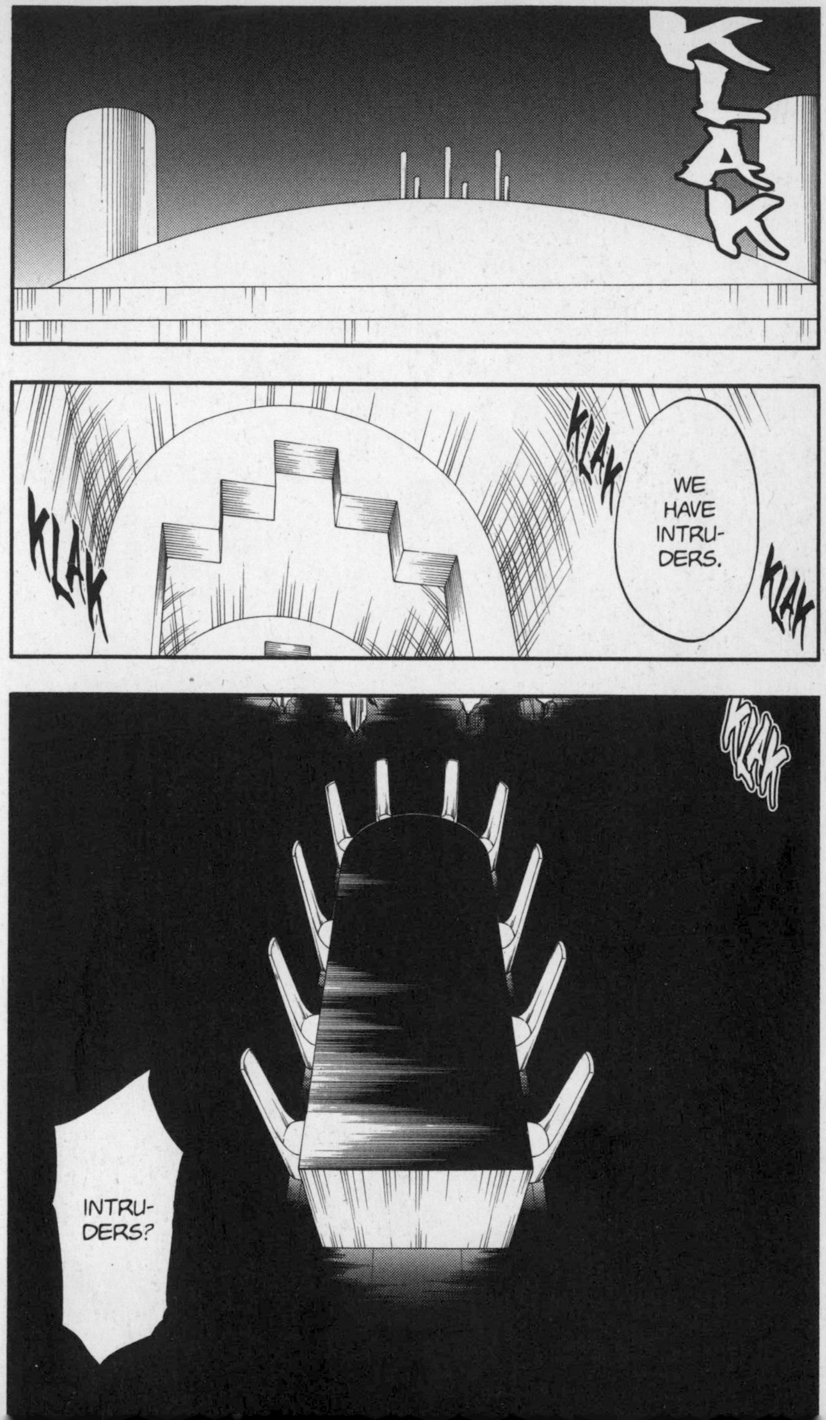

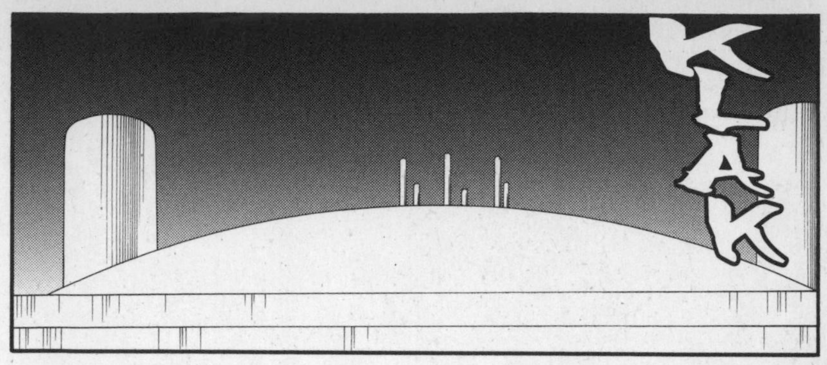

KLAK

INTRUDERS?

UNDER-GROUND PASSAGE #22 HAS SELF-DESTRUCT-ED.
KLA K
OH?!
THEY PICKED AN AWFULLY FAR AWAY SPOT TO BREAK IN.
THUMP
IT WOULD'VE BEEN FUN IF THEY'D BROKEN RIGHT INTO THE THRONE ROOM.
YOU CAN SAY THAT AGAIN.
GLUP
SWUP
SWUP
HA HA!!
SWAK
EXCEL-LENT!!
SHUT UP.
I'M TRYING TO SLEEP OVER HERE. STOP SCREAM-ING.
KREEK
WUMP
THUD
KLAK

TMP

GOOD MORNING...

...ESPADAS.

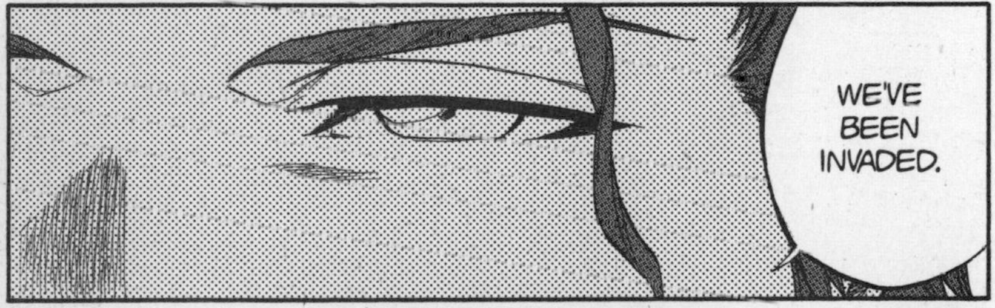

TA—DAH
SAVE KARAKURA
WITH THE KONSÔ
COP KARAKURAIZER
TRANSFORMATION
WATCH!!

245. THE WAY WITHOUT ENEMIES

OUT ENEMIES

BLEACH245

THE WAY WITH

KANAME ...
THE PICTURE PLEASE.
YES, MY LORD.
KLAK
VEEN

SHUK

VWM

OOO OOOO
THERE ARE THREE INTRUDERS.

READ THIS WAY

URYÛ ISHIDA...

...YASUTORA SADO...

...AND ICHIGO KUROSAKI.

!!

THAT'S ...
...THE ENEMY?
PSSH...
YOU SAID IT WAS AN ENEMY RAID.
THOSE ARE JUST KIDS.

THEY LOOK SO...
...BOR-ING.

HMPH

DON'T UNDER-ESTIMATE THEM.
THEY WERE AMONG THE RYOKA THAT INVADED THE SOUL SOCIETY...
...AND DEFIED THE THIRTEEN COURT GUARD COMPANIES.

THERE WERE FOUR THEN.
THEY'RE ONE SHORT THIS TIME.
WHO'S MISSING ?

ORIHIME INOUE.

SO THEY'VE COME TO RESCUE THEIR FRIEND.
I LIKE IT.
BUT THEY LOOK WEAK.

ARE YOU DEAF?
YOU WERE JUST WARNED NOT TO UNDER-ESTIMATE THEM.

I DIDN'T MEAN IT LIKE THAT.
...
DON'T GET YOUR PANTIES IN A BUNCH. ARE YOU AFRAID OF THEM OR SOMETHING?

KLUNK

TMP

WHERE ARE YOU GOING...
...GRIMM-JOW?
I'M GONNA KILL 'EM.
TMP
THEY'RE VERMIN.
THE SOONER THEY'RE EXTER-MINATED THE BETTER.

LORD AIZEN HASN'T GIVEN YOU YOUR ORDERS YET.
SIT DOWN.
...FOR LORD AIZEN.
I'M GOING TO KILL THEM...

GRIMM-
JOW.

...
YES?
YOUR ENTHUSIASM IS APPRE-CIATED.
BUT I HAVEN'T FINISHED TALKING YET.
PLEASE SIT DOWN.

WHAT'S THAT?

I DIDN'T HEAR YOU...
...GRIMMJOW JAEGER-JAQUES.
KRIK
KRIK
KRIK

READ THIS WAY

TOOM

TMP
GOOD.
NOW WE UNDERSTAND EACH OTHER.

HUFF
HUFF
HUFF
NOW THEN...
AS YOU CAN SEE, THREE ENEMIES HAVE ARRIVED.

I WOULDN'T UNDERESTIMATE THEM, BUT THERE'S NO NEED FOR EXCESSIVE ALARM EITHER.
I WANT ALL OF YOU TO RETURN TO YOUR PALACES AND GO ABOUT YOUR BUSINESS AS USUAL.
DON'T BE OVERCONFIDENT...
...AND DON'T BE RECKLESS.
JUST WAIT FOR THE ENEMY.
AND DON'T BE AFRAID.

NO MATTER WHAT HAPPENS...

...AS LONG AS YOU'RE WITH ME...

...NO ONE...

...CAN
DEFEAT
YOU.

HUFF
HUFF
HUFF
HUFF

IT'S NO MIR-AGE.
THERE'S NO WAY WE COULD BE SEEING ONE HERE.
WOULD YOU LIKE ME TO EXPLAIN TO YOU WHAT A MIRAGE IS?
YOU SEE, WHEN HEAT--
NO, THANK YOU!!

SHF SHF SHF SHF SHF SHF SHF

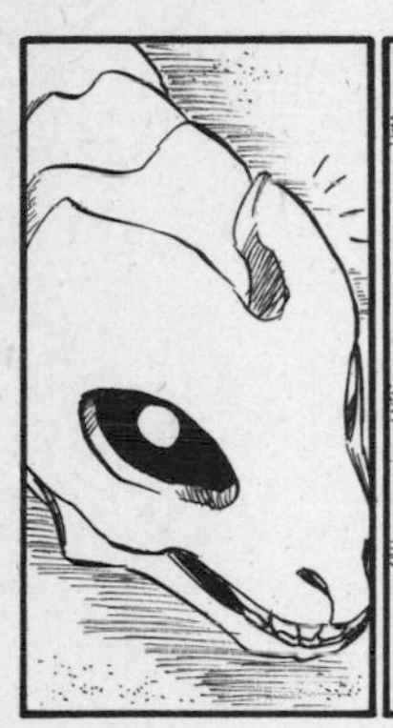

KWSHH
SHF SHF SHF SHF SHF SHF SHF SHF SHF SHF

AT FIRST ...
...I THOUGHT THIS WAS A DEAD WORLD, BUT...
I GUESS IT HAS SOME LITTLE CREATURES IN IT.
EVEN IF THEY'RE JUST HOLLOWS.

BUT DON'T HOLLOWS FEED ON HUMAN SOULS?
SO WHAT DO THESE LITTLE GUYS LIVE ON?
HUECO MUNDO'S ATMOSPHERE HAS A HIGH CONCEN-TRATION OF REISHI.
MAYBE SMALL HOLLOWS CAN SUSTAIN THEMSELVES JUST BY BREATHING.

THERE'S A LOT OF REISHI IN THE ATMO-SPHERE?!
HOW DO YOU KNOW THAT?!
HEH HEH
QUINCIES MAKE USE OF AMBIENT REISHI WHEN THEY FIGHT.
THE HIGHER THE CONCEN-TRATION OF REISHI, THE STRONGER WE ARE.
I REALIZED IT WHEN WE WERE FIGHTING BEFORE.
ONCE I GET THE HANG OF IT, I SHOULD BE ABLE FIGHT EVEN BETTER HERE THAN I DO IN THE WORLD OF THE LIVING OR THE SOUL SOCIETY.

REALLY?
WELL THAT'S CONVENIENT FOR YOU.
YOU AND THE HOLLOWS ARE SET, BUT WHAT ABOUT ME?
WHAT?!!

IT SHOULD BE THE SAME FOR A SOUL REAPER TOO!
HUH?
NOT FOR ME.
WHY NOT YOU?!
THE REISHI IN THE SOUL SOCIETY ENABLED RUKIA TO REGAIN HER SPIRITUAL POWERS!
MAYBE RUKIA'S WEIRD.

READ THIS WAY

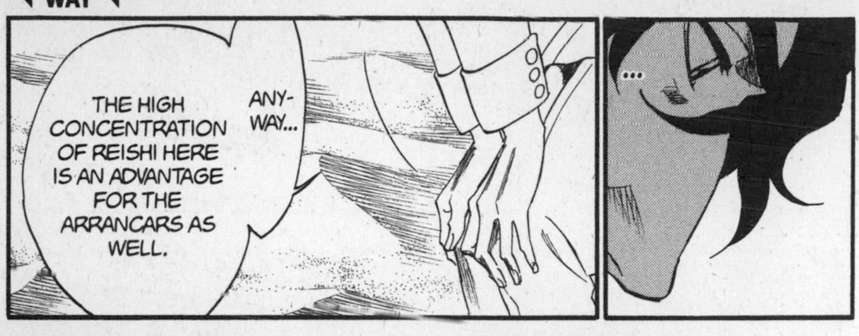
...
ANY-WAY...
THE HIGH CONCENTRATION OF REISHI HERE IS AN ADVANTAGE FOR THE ARRANCARS AS WELL.

I DON'T KNOW HOW CLOSE AIZEN IS TO TURNING HOLLOWS INTO ARRANCARS OR HOW ORGANIZED THEY ARE, BUT...
IN ANY CASE, THE ARRANCARS ARE SURE TO SEE US AS BOTH ENEMIES AND FOOD.
AND WE SHOULD ASSUME THAT ANY HOLLOWS WE MEET HERE ARE SEVERAL TIMES STRONGER THAN THEY APPEAR TO BE.

WE HAVE A LOT TO BE WARY OF.
YOU TALK TOO MUCH.
WE'LL SEE YOU LATER.
THERE YOU GO AGAIN! JUST WHEN I'M...
WHAT-EVER. GO ON, KEEP TALKING.
LET'S GO, CHAD.

HUH?!

NOOOOOO!!

WA HA HA HA HA HA HA HA HA!!

TMP TMP TMP TMP TMP TMP TMP

HUH?
YOU LOOK SO TIRED. WHAT'S WRONG?
WHAT DO YOU THINK? YOU WOKE ME UP!
BUT IT WAS AN ELEGANT WAY TO BE WOKEN UP, WASN'T IT?
ELEGANT?! A VIOLENT ATTACK ACCOMPANIED BY A LITTLE FRENCH ISN'T MY IDEA OF ELEGANCE!!
BON-JOUR! ☆
THUNK

246. The Great Desert Bros.

BWA HA HA HA HA HA HA HA HA !!

TOMP TOMP TOMP TOMP TOM

TWAN

HUH ?!

BOOGA !!

READ THIS WAY

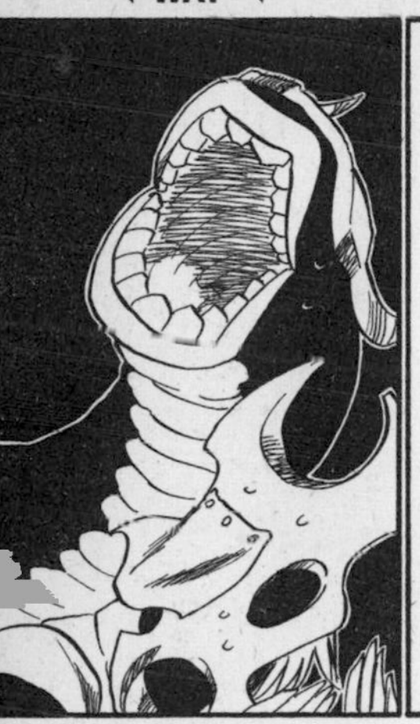

STOP PICKING ON US!!

WE DIDN'T DO ANYTHING TO YOU GUYS!!

A MASK!

ARE YOU...

...A HOLLOW ?!

The Great Desert Bros.

WE'RE SORRY!!
PLEASE FORGIVE US!!

NEL HAD NO IDEA OUR GAME OF ENDLESS TAG WOULD LEAD TO A MISUNDERSTANDING LIKE THIS.
THERE'S NOT A WHOLE LOT TO DO FOR FUN HERE IN HUECO MUNDO.
ENDLESS TAG?
YOU WERE PLAYING?
BUT THERE WERE TEARS IN YOUR EYES.

UH-HUH!
I'M A MASOCHIST, SO IT'S NO FUN FOR ME UNLESS THEY CHASE ME SO HARD I CRY A LITTLE!
WHAT HAVE YOU BEEN TEACHING THIS KID?!
BONK
OOF!!
YOUR NAME IS NEL?

YEAH!

I'M NEL TU OF THE ARRANCARS!

...

THE ARRANCARS?!

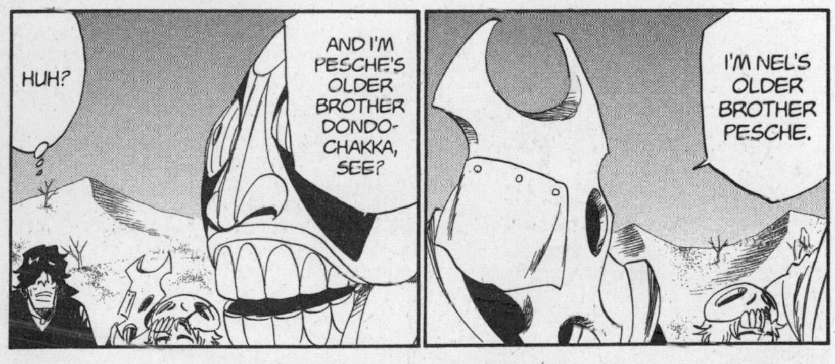

WHAT?
ARRANCARS HAVE FAMILIES AND PETS AND STUFF ?!

HOW RUDE! OF COURSE WE DO!

WE STUMBLED INTO EACH OTHER AND, WELL, SHE WAS SUCH A LITTLE CUTIE-PIE, I FIGURED I COULD BE HER OLDER BROTHER, YA KNOW?
SAME HERE.
THAT DOESN'T MAKE YOU A FAMILY.
HEE HEE. ☆

...!!
TH-THEN WHAT ARE WE ?!
FORGET IT.
MY BAD. YOU'RE A FAMILY.

THIS IS WEIRD.
SHWOSH

ARE YOU GUYS REALLY ARRAN-CARS?
AND HOW COME YOU'RE SITTING ON MY LAP?
WHAT ARE YOU TALKING ABOUT?
CAN'T YOU SEE THIS BEAUTIFUL CRACKED MASK?
BUT YOU GUYS ARE SO DIFFERENT FROM THE ARRANCARS WE MET IN THE WORLD OF THE LIVING.
OH!

OF COURSE WE ARE! THOSE WERE NUMEROS!
NOOMA... HUH? WHAT ARE THEY?
HOP
NUMEROS ARE HIGH-RANKING ARRANCARS!
THEY'RE ASSIGNED A DOUBLE-DIGIT NUMBER AND ARE UNDER THE DIRECT COMMAND OF THE ESPADAS!

NUMEROS ARE EXPERT FIGHTERS!
THEY'RE NOTHING LIKE US GARBAGE BUGS!
GARBAGE BUGS?
COME TO THINK OF IT, YOU GUYS ARE EVEN LESS LIKE ARRANCARS THAN WE ARE!
YOU DON'T HAVE MASKS AND YOU'RE WEARING A BLACK OUTFIT. HA! YOU LOOK MORE LIKE A SOUL...
WHUP

WHA... WHA...
WHAT ARE YOU GUYS?
SHAKE SHAKE SHAKE
ICHIGO KUROSAKI, DEPUTY SOUL REAPER.
URYŪ ISHIDA...
...QUINCY.
YASUTORA SADO ...
...HU-MAN.

AAAAAH! A SOUL REAPER!! BADDIES!!
YOU DIDN'T KNOW WHAT WE WERE?
I SHOULD'VE GUESSED! ARRANCARS DON'T WANT TO GO TO LAS NOCHES!!
THEY'LL KILL US!!
HEEEELP
WAIT... WE'RE NOT GONNA KILL YOU.

SWUFF

THE SOUL REAPER MAY NOT KILL YOU...

...BUT I WILL RIP YOU TO PIECES!

FSHHHHHHHH

I, RUNUGANGA, GUARDIAN OF THE WHITE SAND!!

FSHHHHHH
I JUST RECEIVED WORD FROM LAS NOCHES THAT THERE ARE INTRUDERS IN HUECO MUNDO.
BUT I'M SHOCKED TO FIND YOU PESTS HELPING THEM.

IN-EXCUS-ABLE.
I WILL TURN YOU ALL INTO SAND!
NO! IT'S NOT WHAT YOU THINK!
WE WERE JUST...
MOVE.
HUH?
TMP
GE-TSUGA...

...TEN-SHÔ!!

SHAK

ALL RIGHT, LET'S GO!
AAAAH!!
A SURPRISE ATTACK! YOU CHEATER!
HE'S A BADDIE!!

I JUST SAVED YOUR BUTTS!
ANYWAY, I ATTACKED HIM FROM THE FRONT, SO WHERE'S THE SURPRISE?
SHUFF

PRMMMMMM

YOU ATTACK WITHOUT WARNING AND WITHOUT REMORSE.
INTRUDER...
KSHHHHHH
THAT WAS EVEN MORE...
...IN-EXCUSABLE!

WHOA...

HEY!
WHAT ARE WE GONNA DO?!
URYÛ?!
WHAT DO YOU WANT ME TO DO?
MY ARROWS DON'T KILL SAND.
CHAD?!
I'LL HIT HIM IF YOU WANT, BUT...
JUST RUN!
WE NEED A PLAN! WE GOTTA GET AWAY FROM HIM FOR NOW!!
BAWA! TURN AROUND, BAWA!!

THUD
KREK
YOU...
...WILL...
...NOT...
...ESCAPE!!

WHOA ...
AAAAAH!!
FSHHHHHHHH
FSHHHHH
IT'S AN ANT-LION PIT !!
WE KNOW !!

TSUGI NO MAI. (NEXT DANCE)

HAKUREN. (WHITE WAVE)

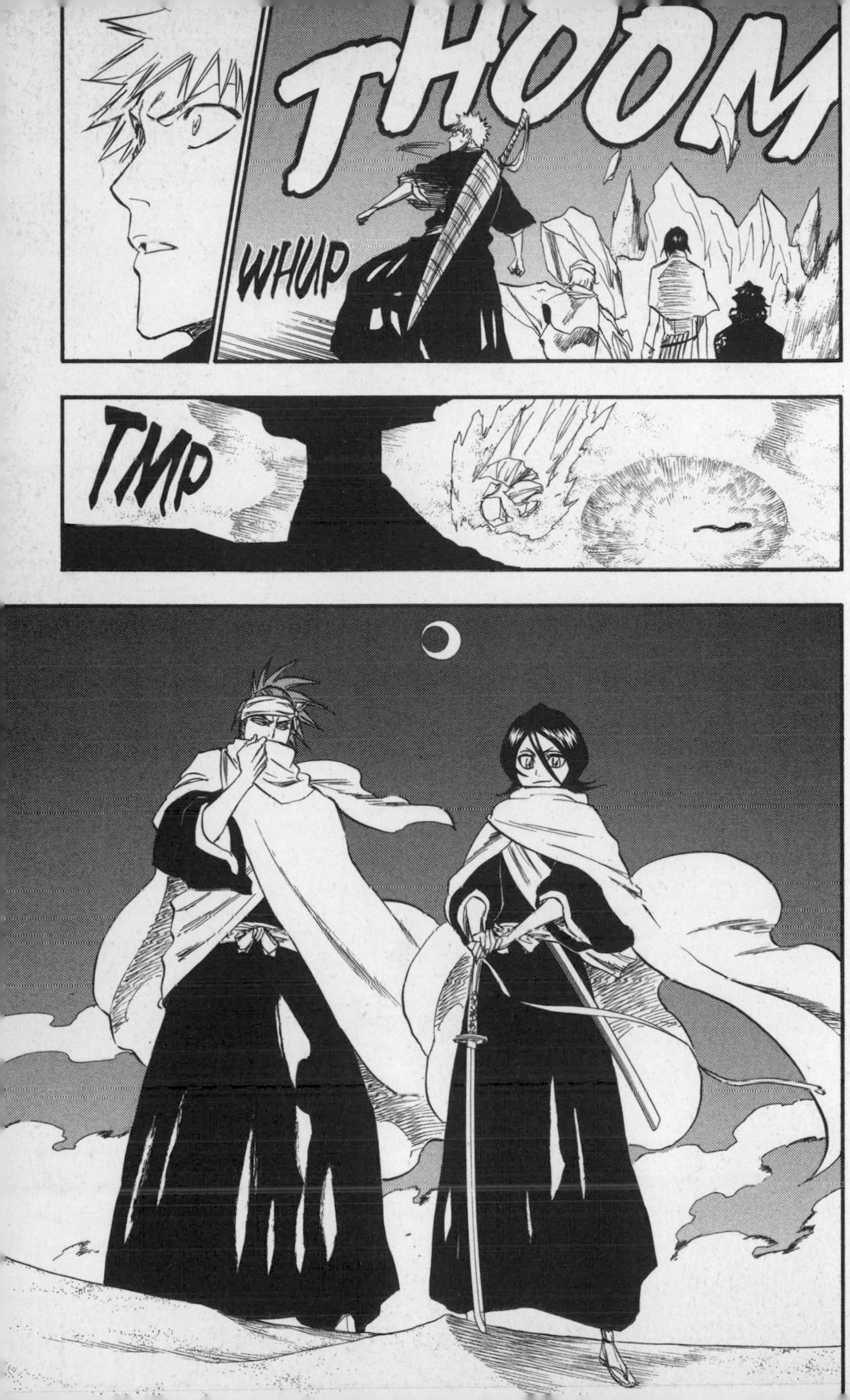

THOOM
WHUP

TMP

NOW, NOW...
HERE. JUST PUT THIS ON AND PRESS THE BUTTON.
YOU'RE GONNA LOVE IT. ♪
FINE.
TRANSFORM...
OH!
CAN YOU PLEASE SAY "CAREER CHANGE"!!
IT'S DESIGNED TO ELECTROCUTE YOU IF YOU SAY ANYTHING ELSE.
WHAT?!
CA...
CAREER CHANGE!!

247. United On The Desert

BLEACH
ブリーチ

247. United On The Desert

BLEACH
ブリーチ

RUKIA!
RENJI!

WHOOM

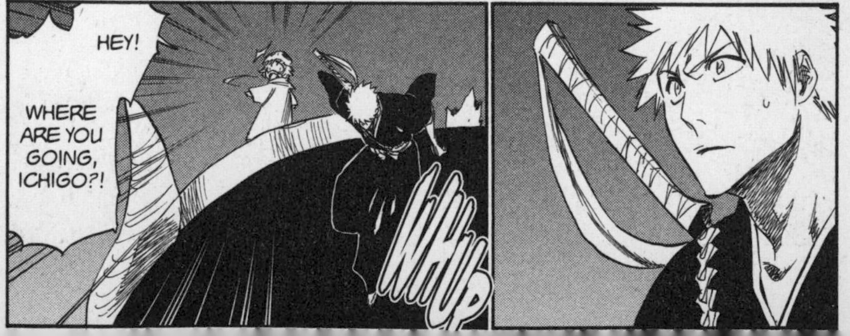

READ THIS WAY

WHAK

OOF!!

THWAK

UGH!!

YOU OKAY, ICHIGO?
YOU IDIOT !!

WHY DID YOU COME TO HUECO MUNDO ?!
WHY DIDN'T YOU WAIT FOR US TO COME BACK?!
'CAUSE... I WASN'T SURE IF YOU GUYS WERE GONNA COME BACK.
WE WOULD'VE COME!!
NO MATTER WHAT IT TOOK!!

STUPID ...
...JERK!
THAT WAS OUR INTENTION FROM THE BEGINNING!
WHY COULDN'T YOU WAIT?

WHY COULDN'T YOU...
...TRUST US?

AREN'T WE...

...YOUR FRIENDS, ICHIGO?

HMPH.
ALL RIGHT THEN.
WHUP
TMP
DON'T EVER MAKE ME...
...ASK YOU THAT AGAIN.

LET'S GO.
GET UP!
AREN'T YOU HERE TO SAVE ORIHIME?

SHWUSHHHHHH
BY THE WAY...
WHAT'S WITH THE CAPES?
WAS THERE A SALE OR SOME-THING?
WE WERE TOLD...
...TO BRING THEM BECAUSE OF THE SAND-STORMS HERE.
BY WHO?

YOU MEAN...

...BYAKUYA SENT YOU TO HUECO MUNDO?!

IT WAS KISUKE WHO OPENED UP THE GARGANTA...

BUT WE WOULDN'T BE HERE IF IT WEREN'T FOR CAPTAIN KUCHIKI.

HE SAID...

"MY ORDERS WERE TO BRING YOU BACK, NOT STOP YOU FROM GOING AGAIN."

"I WAS TOLD TO BRING YOU HERE, NOTHING MORE."
"DO AS YOU PLEASE."

THAT WAS WHAT HE SAID.
WOW.

HMM...
BYAKUYA SAID THAT?
HE SURE HAS MELLOWED OUT.

OH, AND...
HE ALSO SAID, "LET THAT LITTLE PUNK RUN AROUND HUECO MUNDO FOR A WHILE AND SEE HOW THEY LIKE IT."

THAT JERK!
SO...
WHAM
BAWA?!

WHAT ARE THESE GUYS?
HUH?!

WHO...
WHO ARE WE?! WHO ARE YOU?!

I'M NEL TU!!
I'M DON-DO-CHAK-KA!!
PESCHE GUATICHE !!
TO-GETHER WE ARE THE...

HUH?
TA—DAH

I-I THOUGHT WE DECIDED ON PHANTOM THIEF NELDONPE THE OTHER DAY!!
I SAID I WOULDN'T ACCEPT ANYTHING BUT THE GREAT DESERT BROTHERS !!
UNH-UH. IT'S GOTTA BE THE THREE BROTHERS !!
...
THERE YOU GO.
THAT'S HOLLOWS FOR YOU.
I DON'T GET IT.
...
...

BAWA!!
BAWA!!
HEY!!
BAWA-BAWA'S CRYING!!
IT'S OKAY, BAWA-BAWA!!
WE HAVEN'T FORGOTTEN ABOUT YOU!!
C'MON! INCLUDING BAWABAWA, ALL TOGETHER NOW!!
YEAH, OKAY. NOW SHUT UP.
TA-DAH

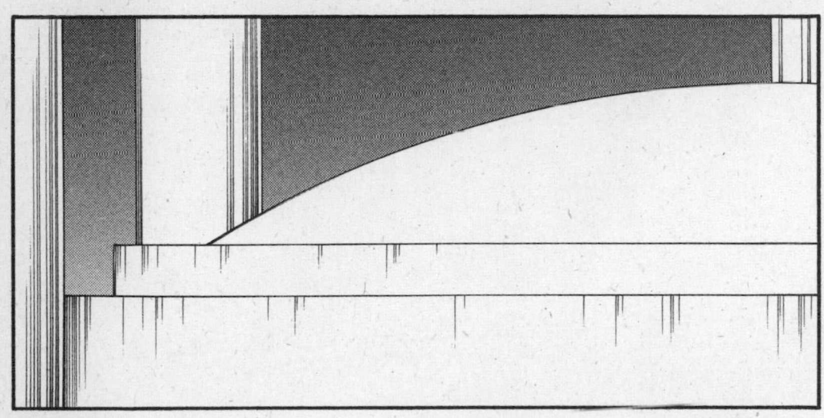

TMP
TMP
TMP

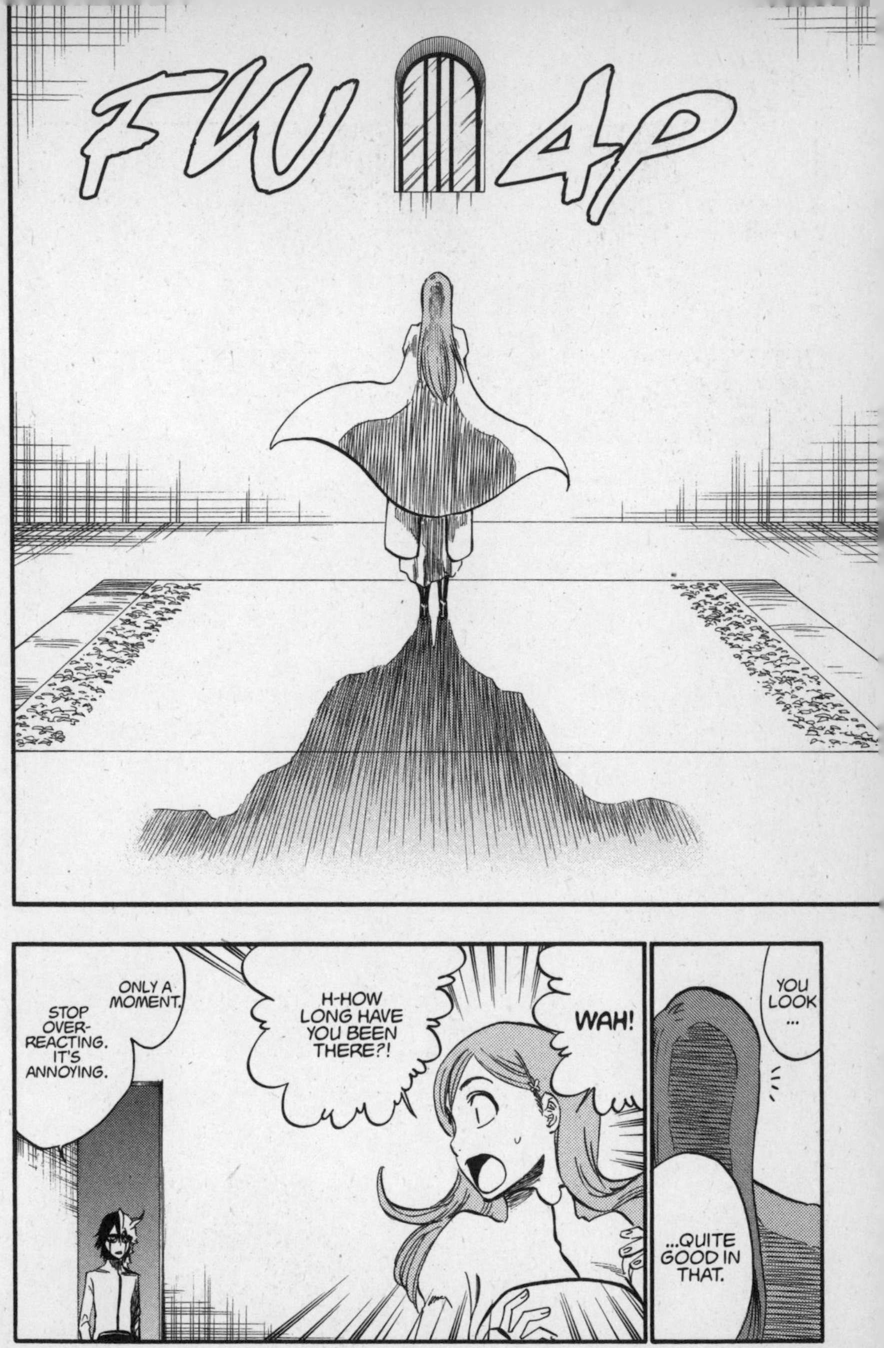

FWAP

YOU LOOK ...
...QUITE GOOD IN THAT.
WAH!
H-HOW LONG HAVE YOU BEEN THERE?!
ONLY A MOMENT.
STOP OVER-REACTING. IT'S ANNOYING.

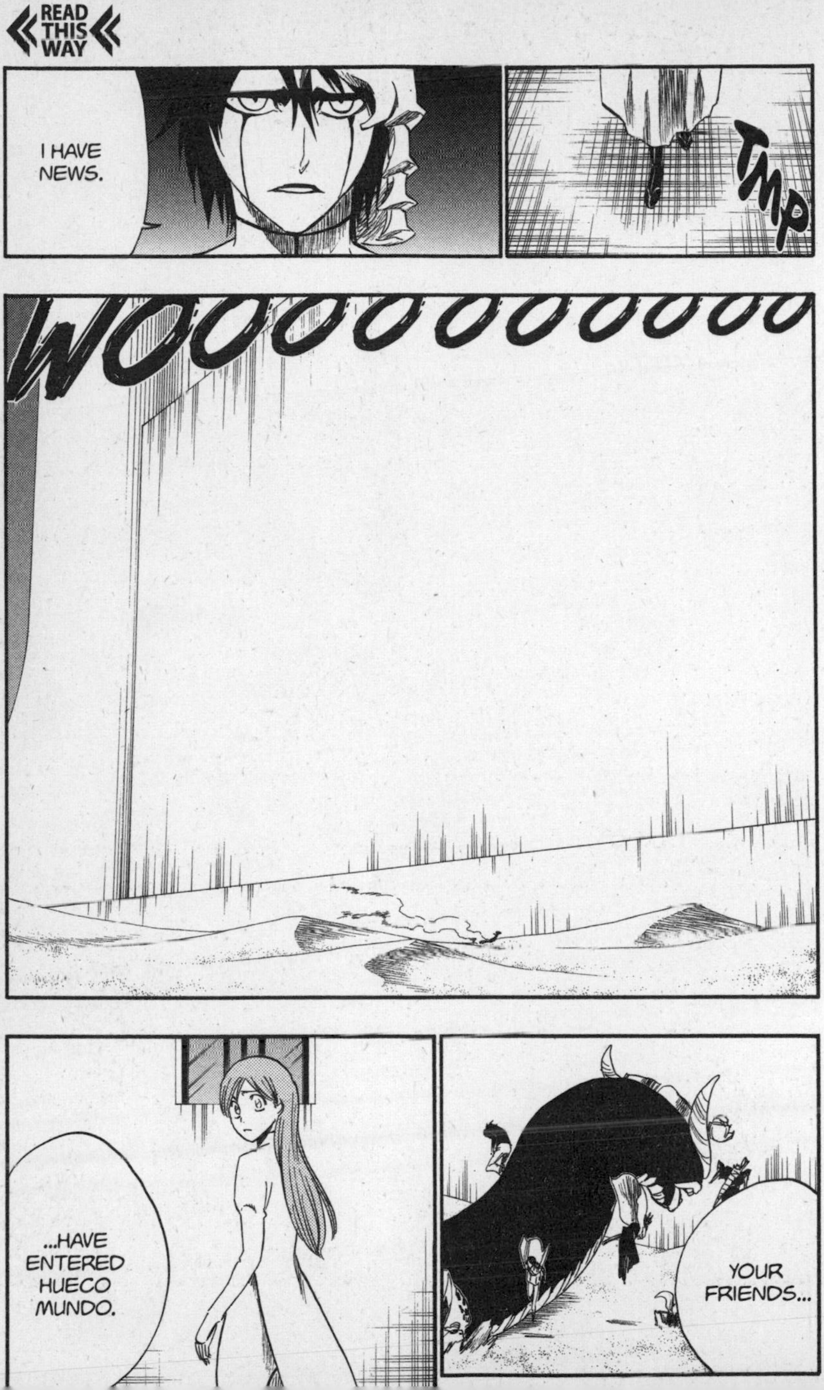

WOOOOOOOOOOO

*AN ORE THAT BLOCKS AND BREAKS DOWN SPIRITUAL ENERGY.

C'MON, RENJI!

WHAP

HEY! YOU'RE NOT THE BOSS HERE!

TO RESCUE YOU, OF COURSE.
WHAT ELSE...
...WOULD BRING THEM HERE?

KLIK
KABOOM
AGH!!
RRMMMM
KOFF
KOFF
RRMMMM
GACK
THERE HE IS.
KARAKURA'S NEW HERO.

248. Alive and Back Here Once Again

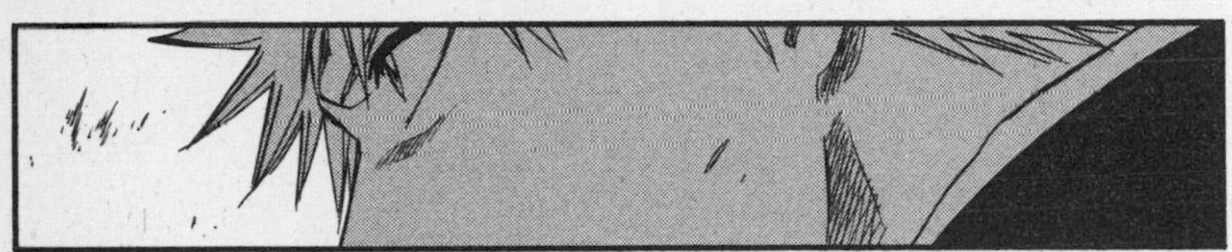

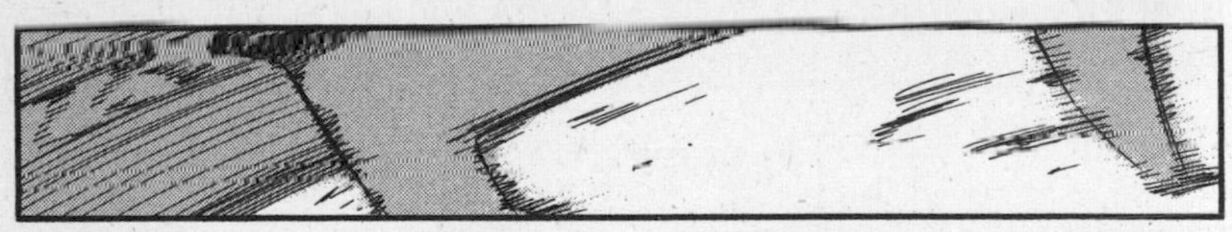

THAT'S WHAT THE GARMENT YOU'RE WEARING SIGNIFIES...
...ORIHIME INOUE.

YES.

SAY IT.

YOUR BODY AND SPIRIT...

WHAT ARE THEY FOR?

YES.

248. Alive and Back Here Once Again

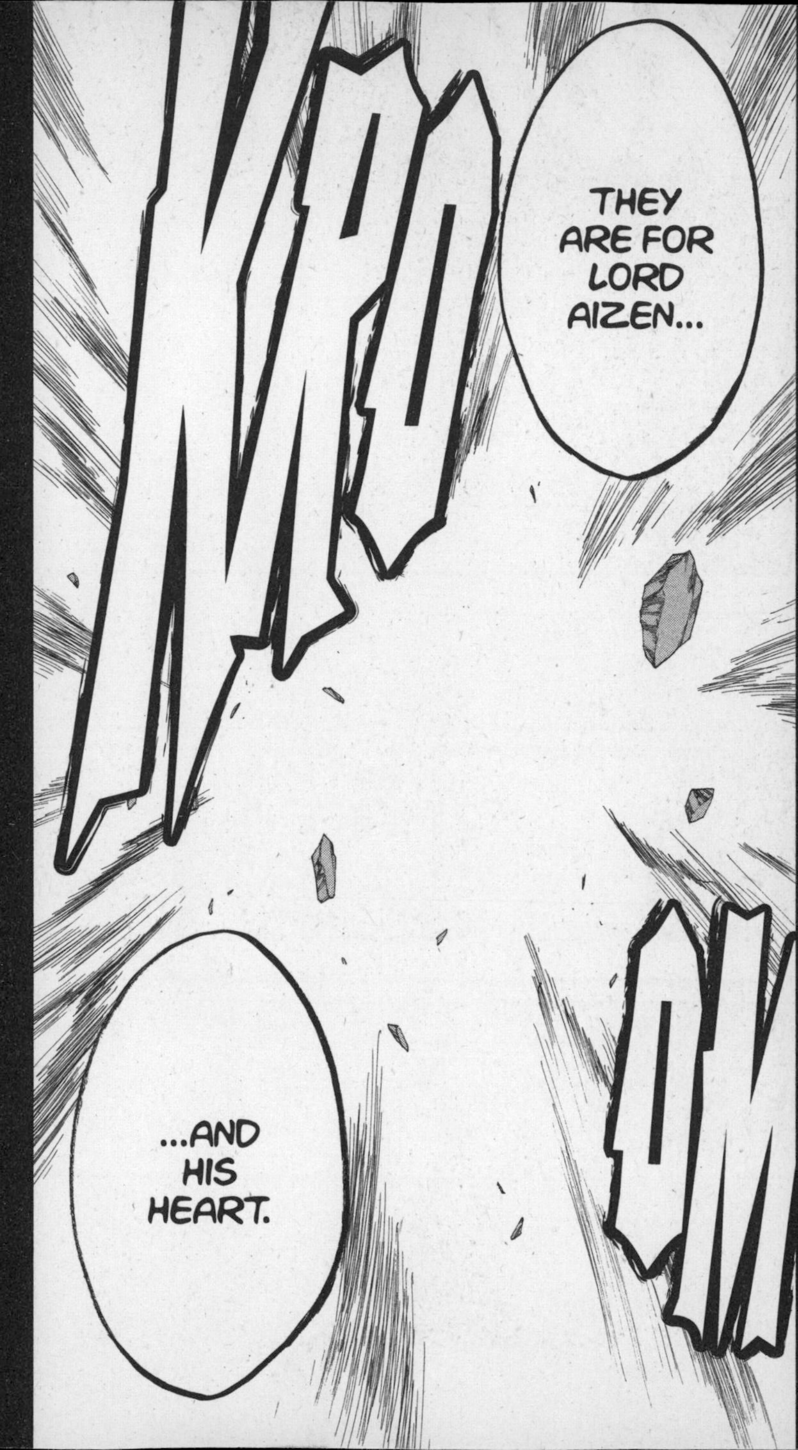

THEY ARE FOR LORD AIZEN...

...AND HIS HEART.

KROOSH

OOOOOOOOOOOO
DID WE GET THROUGH?
I THINK SO.
I FEEL A BREEZE.
WHA...

WHY DID YOU DO THAT?!
THE GATE'S ONLY A THREE-DAY WALK FROM HERE!
WAKE UP, KID.
WE'RE NOT VISITING A FRIEND HERE. WE CAN'T JUST WALK IN THROUGH THE FRONT DOOR.
AND WE DON'T HAVE THREE DAYS.
NEL...

THANK YOU...
...FOR BRINGING US HERE.

WE BECAME TRAITORS...
...THE MOMENT RUNUGANGA FOUND US!!
MAY-BE...
...EVEN BEFORE THAT!
LORD AIZEN MAY HAVE KNOWN FROM THE START!

HE'LL NEVER FORGIVE US!!
AND EVEN IF HE DID, THE ESPADAS WON'T!
IF YOU DON'T TAKE US WITH YOU, WE'LL BE KILLED!!
YOU HAVE TO TAKE US!
IF YOU DON'T...
SOB

I'LL CRY!!
BLUB
BWAAA!!!

I-ICHIGO, YOU MEANIE!!
CARROT TOP!!
DOO-DOO HEAD!!
ALL RIGHT, ALL RIGHT! STOP CRYING!!
STINKY BREATH!
HEY, THAT'S NOT TRUE!!
WHAT'S ALL THE YELLING ABOUT?
VIRGIN!!
SHUT UP!!!

TMPTMPTMP

TMPTMPTMPTMPTMPTMP
THIS WALL'S SO THICK.
HOW FAR DOES THIS TUNNEL GO?
AND IT'S DARK. I CAN'T SEE ANYTHING.
HEH...
NO PROBLEM. I'LL TAKE CARE OF THAT.

WHAT? WHAT'RE YOU GONNA DO?
JUST SHUT UP AND WATCH.
WITH A LITTLE CREATIVITY, KIDÔ CAN DO SOME AMAZING THINGS.
HADÔ 31...
SHAKKAHÔ! (RED FLAME CANNON)
FW
OOM

FWIK FWIK FWUT
TMPTMPTMP
...
WOW.
AN INCREDIBLY SMALL LIGHT.
AND I THOUGHT YOU WERE GONNA SHOW OFF.

*A DESTRUCTION CHANT, OR POWERFUL KIDÔ.

A CROSS-ROADS ?!

NOW WHAT?

I THINK IT'S REALLY TIME TO SAY GOODBYE NOW.
NEL...

KREK

I DON'T THINK YOU GUYS...

...CAN HANDLE THE SPIRITUAL PRESSURE BEYOND THIS POINT.

KREK

FIVE PATHS.
WE'LL HAVE TO TRY THEM ALL.
NO.

EACH OF US...
...SHOULD TAKE A DIFFERENT PATH.

...
BUT...

ARE YOU CRAZY?! WE'RE UP AGAINST ESPADAS HERE!!
WE CAN'T DIVIDE OUR FORCE !!

AND THERE'S NO GUARANTEE THEY'LL COME AT US ONE AT A TIME!
IF WE SPLIT UP...

TMP
DON'T.

IT'S INSULTING TO A WARRIOR...

...TO HAVE SOMEONE WORRY ABOUT HIS WELFARE.

CHARM?

YEAH.

IT'S AN OLD TRADITION.

THE THIRTEEN COURT GUARD COMPANIES USED TO DO ONE BEFORE A BIG BATTLE.

WE DON'T DO IT MUCH ANYMORE, BUT...

...I THOUGHT THIS MIGHT BE A GOOD TIME TO REVIVE THE TRADITION.

ALL RIGHT, HOLD OUT YOUR HANDS!

DON'T LOOK AT ME LIKE THAT! I'M EMBARRASSED ENOUGH!

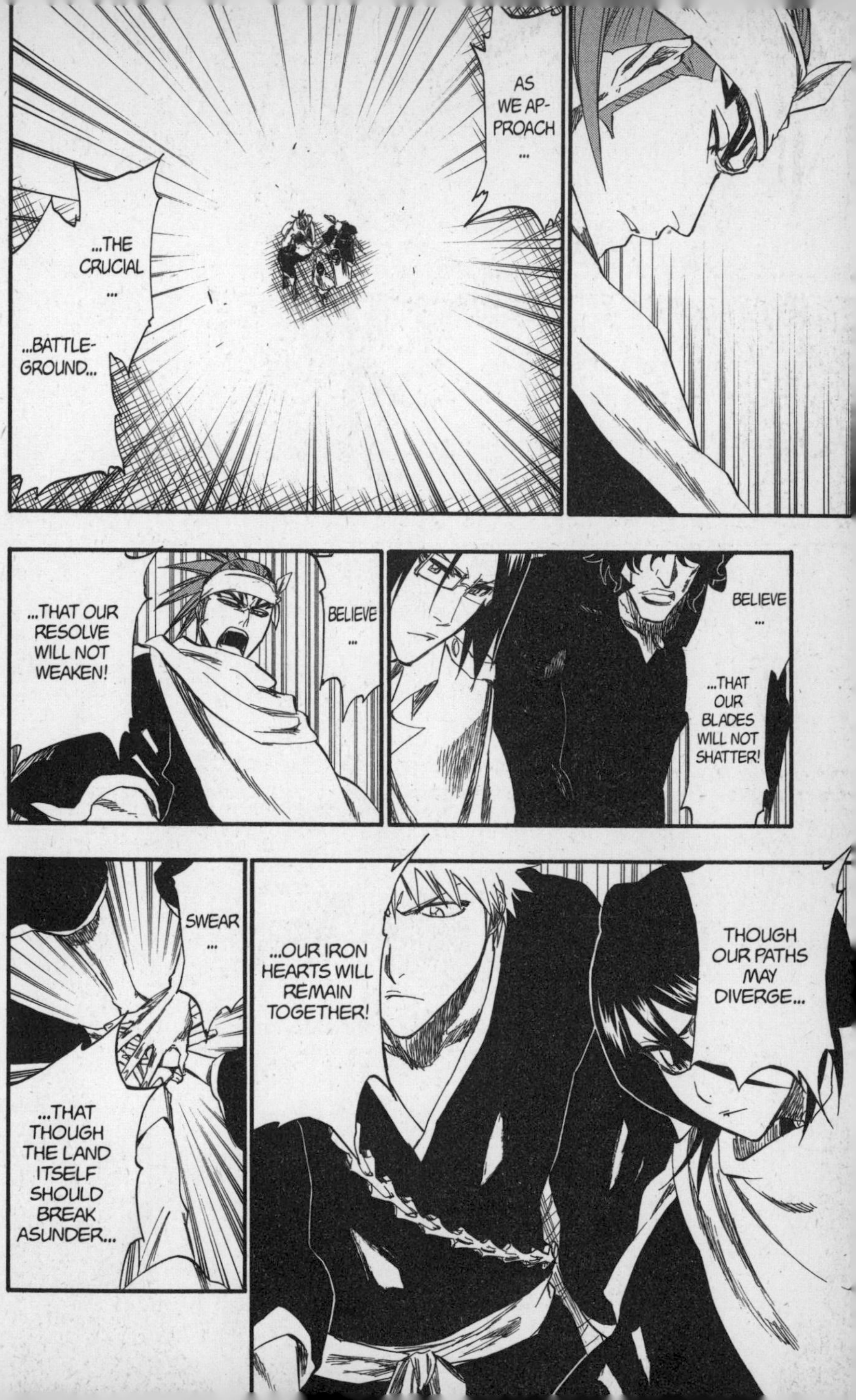

AS WE AP-PROACH ...
...THE CRUCIAL ...
...BATTLE-GROUND...

WE WILL ...
...COME BACK HERE...
...ALIVE !!

YOU

KONSÔ COP KARA-KURAIZER !!
TA-DAH
YUCK!!

249. Back to the Innocence

THEY AMM-SCRAYED.
...

ICHIGO?
YEAH!
I HAD FUN COMING HERE!!
LOTS AND LOTS OF FUN!!
I...
...WANT TO STAY WITH ICHIGO!!

NEL!!
SHO OM

ALL RIGHT! WE'LL...
WHU P
...GO TOO!!

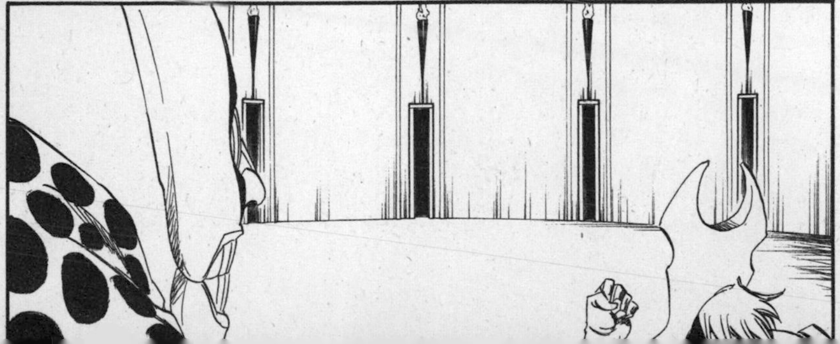

WHICH WAY DID SHE GO?

WHICH ONE WAS IT?

BLEACH 249.

Back to the Innocence

READ THIS WAY

HOW DID IT GO?

HOW'S OUR LITTLE PET DOING?

DON'T BE ANGRY.
KREK
I JUST WANT TO KNOW IF EVERY-THING'S GOING WELL.
IS IT?

DON'T WORRY.
THE GIRL WAS...
...IN LORD AIZEN'S POWER BEFORE SHE EVER GOT HERE.

...
HE USED KYÔKA SUIGE-TSU?

PLEASE.
THERE WAS NO NEED.

WHEN WE INVITED HER HERE...
...WE PUT HER IN A MULTI-LAYERED PSYCHIC CAGE.

I TOLD HER THAT HER FRIENDS WOULD DIE IF SHE RESISTED IN ANY WAY.
THEN I GAVE HER A 12-HOUR FURLOUGH.
I ALLOWED HER TO SAY A SILENT AND INVISIBLE GOODBYE TO JUST ONE OF HER FRIENDS.

THAT WAS YOUR CAGE?

READ THIS WAY

BY GIVING HER A REPRIEVE WHEN SHE WAS IN A STATE OF TERROR...
...AND LETTING HER BID FAREWELL TO A FRIEND...
...I LED HER TO FALSELY BELIEVE THAT WE WERE SYMPATHETIC TO HER.
THAT WEAK-ENED HER WILL.

IN FACT, THE FURLOUGH WAS A DECEPTION, A WAY TO CONFUSE HER FACULTIES.
BY ALLOWING HER TO CHOOSE WHO SHE WOULD SAY GOODBYE TO...
...WE CREATED THE ILLUSION THAT SHE WAS ACTING OF HER OWN VOLITION RATHER THAN BEING ABDUCTED.

AND BY ALLOWING HER TO RETURN TO THE RENDEZVOUS ON HER OWN RECOGNI-ZANCE...
...BEFORE BRINGING HER HERE...
...THAT ILLUSION WAS DEEPLY INGRAINED IN HER PSYCHE.
HER WILL TO ESCAPE WAS DE-STROYED.
...
AND...

WHEN SHE SAID HER SECRET GOODBYE...
...A FAINT TRACE OF HER DEPARTURE WAS LEFT WITH ONE OF HER FRIENDS.
SO WHAT?
WASN'T THAT A MISTAKE?

QUITE THE OPPO-SITE.
THAT VESTIGE OF HER DEPARTURE ...
...PROVES THAT SHE HAD FREEDOM OF MOVEMENT AND THOUGHT UNTIL THE MOMENT OF HER SURRENDER.

IN OTHER WORDS ...
...BECAUSE OF THAT TRACE...
...HER ACTIONS APPEAR TO HER FRIENDS TO BE A VOLUNTARY BETRAYAL.

I DON'T KNOW IF IT WAS A COMPLETE SUCCESS.
BUT IT'S SAFE TO SAY THAT THE SOUL SOCIETY HAS ABANDONED HER.

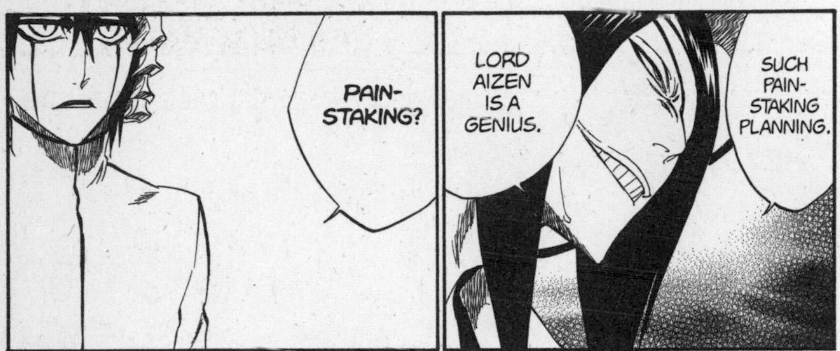
SUCH PAIN-STAKING PLANNING.
LORD AIZEN IS A GENIUS.
PAIN-STAKING?

TO LORD AIZEN...
...IT WAS JUST A GAME.
IF IT WORKED, FINE.
IF IT DIDN'T, SO BE IT.

NONE-THELESS...
...RIGHT NOW, THE GIRL HASN'T GOT THE WILL...
...TO EVEN ATTEMPT AN ESCAPE.

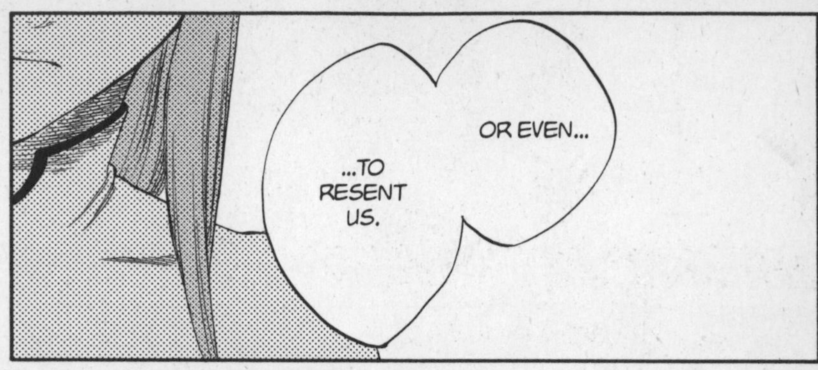
OR EVEN...
...TO RESENT US.

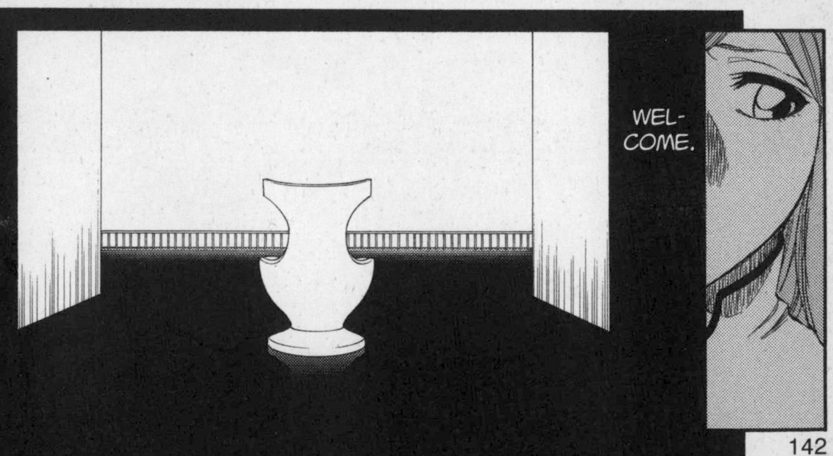
WEL-
COME.

ORIHIME...
THANK YOU FOR COMING.
THERE'S SOMETHING I WANT TO SHOW YOU.
LOLY...
MEN-OLY...
EXCUSE US.
SIR?
B-BUT...
WE CAN'T LEAVE YOU ALONE WITH THIS GIRL!
FOR-
FORGIVE US, MASTER!!
BOW

THAT STUPID LITTLE WITCH!
KLAK
WELL NOW ...

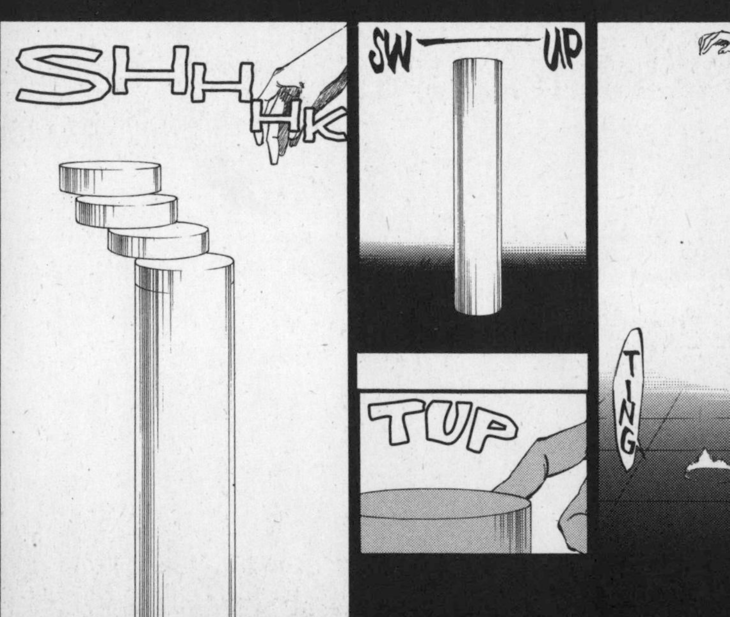

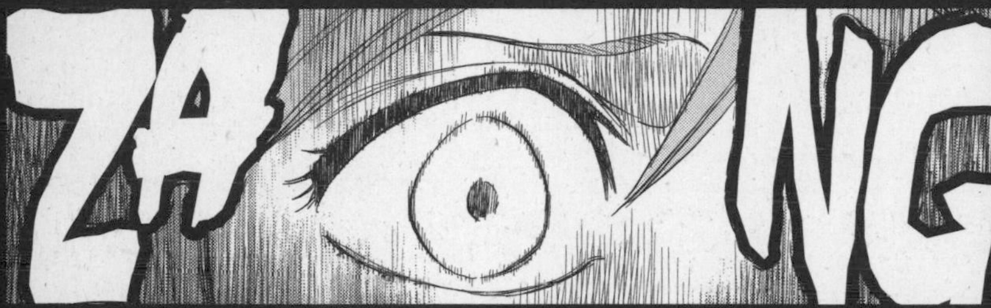
ZA
NG

WHAT'S THIS SENSATION?
IS THAT...?

SO YOU RECOGNIZE IT.
YES, THIS IS THE HÔGYOKU.

ITS SLEEP HAS BEEN DISRUPTED A NUMBER OF TIMES LATELY, SO IT'S A BIT WEAK RIGHT NOW...
WMM
WMM
BUT IT'S MAKING STEADY PROGRESS. IT WILL FULLY AWAKEN SOON.

TURNING HOLLOWS INTO ARRAN-CARS...
THE CREATION OF THE ÔKEN...
NEITHER WOULD BE POSSIBLE WITHOUT THE HÔGYOKU.
I'M SHOWING YOU THIS...
...SO YOU'LL KNOW THAT I TRUST YOU.
YOUR ABILITY, THE REJECTION OF PHENOMENA...
...THE DENIAL OF EVENTS...
...THE DESTRUCTION OF A PHENOMENON ITSELF...
...IS A TREMENDOUS POWER.
I...
...NEED YOUR HELP.
ORI-HIME...
YOU WILL USE THAT ABILITY OF YOURS...
...TO HELP ME, WON'T YOU?

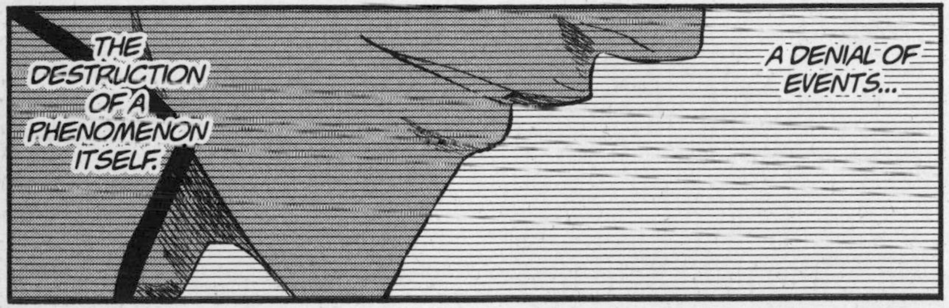

IT'S SOME-THING...

...ONLY I CAN DO.

THE PHENOMENON I HAVE TO DESTROY...

...IS THE HÔGYOKU!

I HAD MR. ISHIDA DESIGN IT. ♪
HE WAS THE WORST POSSIBLE CHOICE!!!

250. Five Ways To Three Figures
TMP
TMP TMP TMP TMP TMP TMP TMP TMP
TMP TMP TMP TMP
TMP
TMP
EE...
EEE...
WHAT ?!

ICHIGO!!!

BLEACH 250. Five Ways to Three Figures

SHE EN
SUPER ACCELER-ATION!
THUNK
WHOOF!!

READ THIS WAY

I-
ICHIGO?
WHAT'S WRONG?
BE QUIET!
...
COME OUT HERE!

WHO-EVER IT IS HIDING UP THERE...
SHOW YOUR-SELF!!

WHOOSH
!
STOP!

YOU CAN'T GET AWAY FROM ME!
HMPH.
WHO'S RUNNING...
TMP TMP TMP TMP TMP TMP

...AWAY ?!
SWIP

KRASH
AGH !!

...
KLAK KLAK
KLAKKLAKKLAK
THUD

UM...
FWOOF FWOOF
KLUNK
HELLO?
YOU OKAY?

WOBBLE
RRMMMMMM

DA-DAH!!!
FWUP
ZANG

DUNT-DA-DA DA-DUNT-DA-DAAA...
FWUP
FWUP
FWUP
DA-DA...
DUNT-DA...
KOFF!
KOFF!
KOFF!
KOFF!
DA-DAAN...
KOFF!
FWUP
FWUP

SHEEN

HEY!!

TA-DAH

NOW...
HEY, YOU!!
EEN

WELL, I...
WHAT'S THAT LOOK FOR?!
WHAT IS THAT ?!
WHAT'S THAT LOOK FOR?!
YEAH, I HEARD YOU THE FIRST TIME.

YOU WITNESSED DORDONI'S GRAND ENTRANCE AND YET...
GRAND? YOU FELL ON YOUR FACE.
...YOU FEIGN COMPOSURE!!
I'M NOT FEIGNING. I'M ACTUALLY COMPOSED.
ALL RIGHT, BUT WHAT ABOUT THE LITTLE ONE BEHIND YOU! THAT KID'S NOT EVEN LOOKING AT ME!!
HMPH. FINE.
THIS JUST SHOWS THAT YOU HAVE NO APPRECIATION FOR THE FINER THINGS.
IT'S REALLY IRRELEVANT SINCE YOU'RE ABOUT TO BE DEMOLISHED ANYWAY.

NOW BRACE YOURSELF, SOUL REAPER...

...FOR ARRANCAR NO. 103!

DORDONI...

...IS GOING TO CRUSH YOU RIGHT NOW!!

TMP

MISTER...

YOU SEEM... KIND OF WIMPY.

WHAT?!

I'LL SHOW YOU WIMPY!!

BUT DON'T CRY ABOUT IT LATER, NIÑO!!!

WHAT?

ARE YOU INTO PEEPING NOW?

THAT'S NOT VERY NICE...
...TÔSEN.

WATCH YOUR MOUTH.
YOU CAME HERE TO CATCH A GLIMPSE OF THEM TOO, DIDN'T YOU...
...ICHI-MARU?

TMP
TAKE IT EASY.
I WAS JUST KIDDING.
DON'T BE SO GROUCHY.
WHAP

UH, TÔSEN...
CAN YOU DO SOMETHING ABOUT THIS KID?
WONDER-WEISS.

RRR...
CHOMP
SO THE LITTLE FREAK'S TAKEN A LIKING TO YOU, EH?
THE PURE ARE DRAWN TO EACH OTHER.
THOUGH I HAVE YET TO DISCOVER WHAT THIS BOY'S PURITY IS DIRECTED TOWARD.

I SEE.
NO WONDER HE DOESN'T LIKE ME.
ANY SANE PERSON WOULD BE LEERY OF YOU.
ANYWAY, TAKE A LOOK AT THIS.
THEY'VE...
...SPLIT UP.

*SPANISH FOR "THREE DIGITS."

READ THIS WAY
?!
ICHIGO !!
WHAT THE ...!!
TRES ...?
YES.

GETSUGA TENSHÔ !!!

A THREE-DIGIT NUMBER IS...
...A SIGN OF DEMOTION.
IT DE-NOTES...
...ESPADAS WHO'VE BEEN DIVESTED OF THEIR RANK.
WE CALL...
...THOSE WITH THREE-DIGIT NUMBERS...

...PRIVARON
ESPADAS.
HEY
...
DIDN'T
YOUR
MAMA
EVER
TEACH
YOU...

...NOT TO JUDGE A BOOK BY ITS COVER...
...NIÑO?

REEOWW
REEOWW
...?
IS THAT A CAT?
POOF
THE ALARM!!
A HOLLOW!!
HOLD ON, KON!!
I MEAN...
KARA-KURA KONSÔ COP!!
WHAT WILL HAPPEN TO THE KONSÔ COP?!
UM... JUST CALL ME KON.
TO BE CONTINUED

251. Baron's Lecture 1st Period

...USED TO BE ESPADAS...

...NIÑO.

BLEACH 251. Baron's Lecture 1st Period

THWAM
SHH
UNH...

TMPTMP
TMPTMPTMPTMP
HA HA!
WHAT'S WRONG?!
SHOOM

KRO

BOOM

READ
THIS
WAY

!
LOOKING DOWN?
YOU SHOULDN'T HAVE TO LOOK TO KNOW WHERE YOU'RE GOING TO LAND.

THWA

TUMP

SNORT

SLOW REFLEXES, A POROUS DEFENSE...

...PATHETIC SPATIAL AWARENESS...

READ THIS WAY

NO WAY.
KRESH

WHY NOT?

A PRIVARON ESPADA...
...ISN'T REALLY AN ESPADA, RIGHT?
KLAK
KLAK

...
CORRECT.

I'VE GOT TO BEAT ALL THE ESPADAS IN HUECO MUNDO.
SO I CAN'T BE WASTING MY BANKAI...
KLANK

...ON SOMEBODY WHO'S NOT EVEN AN ESPADA !!

I SEE.

I UNDER-
STAND
PERFECTLY,
NIÑO.

BUT
ALLOW
ME...

...TO GIVE
YOU SOME
ADVICE.

DON'T UNDER-ESTIMATE ME.

...GIRALDA!
(STORM BARON)
CRAP!
HE CAN RELEASE IT WITHOUT EVEN DRAWING HIS SWORD?!
WHAT ARE YOU DOING?
RAISE YOUR WEAPON.

WHAT ?!

READ THIS WAY
ARE YOU READY?

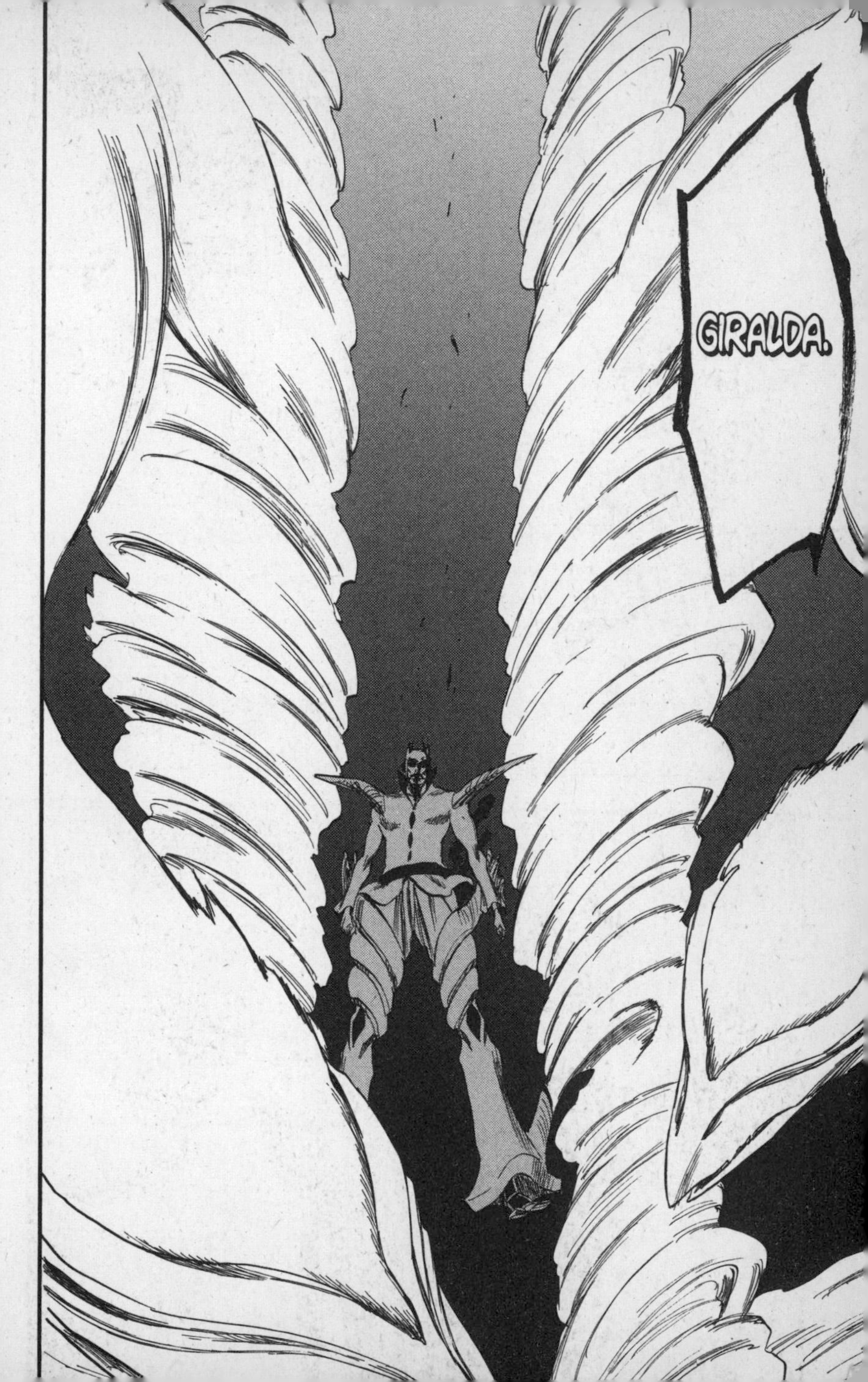
GIRALDA.

HMF !!

KREK

Next Volume Preview

The closer Ichigo and the rescue team get to Aizen's lair, the stronger their Arrancar opponents get. Pushed to the limit, can Ichigo, Uryû and Chad take their power to the next level…or will they crash and burn?

Read it first in SHONEN JUMP magazine!

RRMMMMMMMMMMM